GENETICS

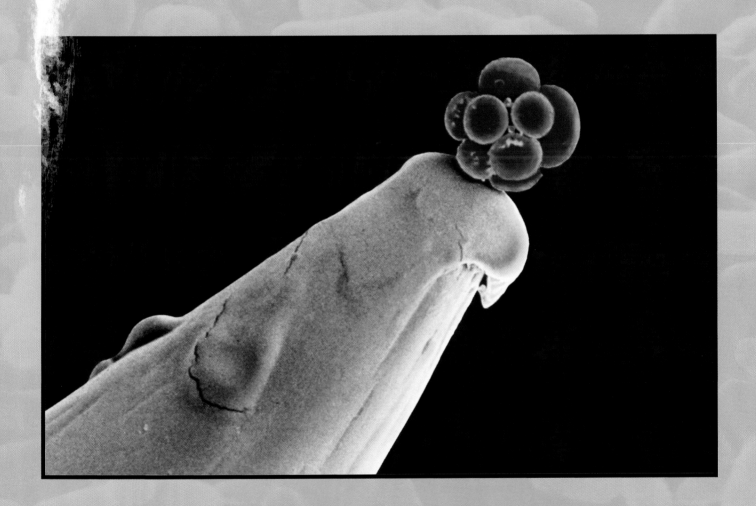

ANNA CLAYBOURNE

Evans

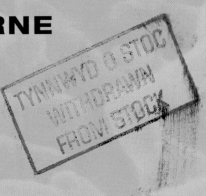

TITLES IN THE SCIENCE IN FOCUS SERIES:
DIGITAL TECHNOLOGY   THE EARTH'S RESOURCES   GENETICS
THE HUMAN BODY   THE SOLAR SYSTEM   WEATHER

Produced for Evans Brothers Limited by
Monkey Puzzle Media Limited
Gissing's Farm, Fressingfield
Suffolk IP21 5SH, UK

Published by Evans Brothers Limited
2A Portman Mansions
Chiltern Street
London W1U 6NR

First published 2006
© copyright Evans Brothers 2006

VISIT OUR WEBSITE
Evans
www.evansbooks.co.uk

British Library Cataloguing in Publication Data
Claybourne, Anna
Genetics – (Science in focus)
1.Genetics– Juvenile literature
I.Title
576.5

ISBN 0 237 52724 3
13-digit ISBN (from 1 January 2007) 978 0 237 52724 2

Editor: Steve Parker
Designer: Jane Hawkins
Picture researcher: Lynda Lines
Artwork by Michael Posen

Picture acknowledgements:
Empics 40 (Lindomar Cruz/Agencia Brasil/AP); Getty Images front cover top left (Dr Dennis
Kunkel/Visuals Unlimited), 6 (Jeff Hunter/The Image Bank), 15 (CMSP/Science Faction), 21 bottom
(Cobalt Stock/Iconica), 25 (Dr Stanley Flegler/Visuals Unlimited), 27 bottom (Ken Weaver/America
24/7), 35 top (Dr TJ Beveridge/Visuals Unlimited), 37 (Dr Dennis Kunkel/Visuals Unlimited), 41 bottom
(Robert Nickelsberg); Nature Picture Library 41 top (Bristol City Museum); Photolibrary.com 7 both
(Phototake), 17 bottom (Colin Milkins/OSF), 32 (Dr Derek Bromhall); Rex Features 19 (Roger Bamber),
20 (Geoff Wilkinson), 24 (Alix/Phanie), 31 (SIPA), 33, 35 bottom (Burger/Phanie), 36 (Alix Phanie);
Science Photo Library front cover main image (BSIP Laurent), front cover centre left (Pasieka), 3 (Dr
Yorgos Nikas), 8 (Carlyn Iverson), 9 (Andrew Syred), 10 (Pasieka), 11 (Philippe Psaila), 12 (Steve
Gschmeissner), 16 (Christian Darkin) 17 top (Art Wolfe), 18 (Dr Yorgos Nikas), 22 (Adam Hart-Davis),
28 (James King-Holmes), 29 top (A Barrington Brown), 34 (Maximilian Stock Ltd); Still Pictures 13
bottom (M & C Denis-Huot), 14 (Ed Reschke), 21 top (Hartmut Schwarzbach), 26 (Shehzad Noorani),
27 top (Laura Dwight), 29 bottom (CSHL Archives), 38 (Joerg Boethling), 39 (Adrian Arbib).

CONTENTS

THE KEY TO LIFE

Genes are the key to life on Earth. They are far too small to see. But all living things, from whales and humans to worms and tiny germs, have genes inside them. Genes control the way their bodies grow and work.

WHAT ARE GENES?

All living things are made up of microscopic 'building blocks' called cells. The tiniest creatures and plants consist of a few hundred cells. Bigger living things like humans, horses and trees contain many billions of cells. Genes are tiny groups of chemicals found inside these microscopic cells. The genes work like instructions, telling each cell how to grow and do its job. By controlling cells, genes control the way a whole living thing works, what it looks like and how it survives.

Each main kind, or species, of living thing has its own set of genes which make it different from other species. For example, a goldfish's

▲ Colourful fish and other creatures swim around a coral reef – one of the world's richest places for wildlife. Each animal's genes help to determine what that animal looks like – its body shape, colours and patterns – as well as how its body works inside.

genes make it grow into a goldfish. Human genes make us grow into human beings. Also, within a species, genes make each individual look slightly different. For example, all people have the basic set of human genes for the human species. But small differences between the genes of different people affect each person's eye colour, hair type, skin colour, overall height, face shape, ear shape and many other body features.

▲ A scientist who studies genes is called a geneticist. This geneticist is at work in her laboratory, comparing seeds of the genetically altered plants she is growing as part of her research.

GENES AND DNA

The cells inside the bodies of living things are too small to see. About 50 in a row would stretch across the dot on this 'i'. Genes are found inside cells, and are even tinier. Genes are made of a chemical substance called DNA. This is in the form of long string-like pieces, or strands, inside each cell.

UNDERSTANDING GENES

Because genes are so tiny, for a long time scientists did not know that they existed. We have only really begun to understand genes in the last hundred years or so. Compared to other sciences, the science of genes – called genetics – is quite new. But we are finding out fast about genes, how they work and how we can change them. We are also finding many new uses for genes, from curing diseases and making medicines to catching criminals and helping threatened wildlife.

A CLOSER LOOK

The first microscopes, built in the seventeenth century, allowed scientists to see the tiny cells in living things for the first time. But these microscopes were not powerful enough to see the long pieces or strands of DNA that form genes. From the 1880s better microscopes could magnify by thousands of times. They revealed the strands of DNA inside cells.

▼ All living things are made of microscopic cells. These adipose cells from the human body are specialised to store fat. They are shown about 1,000 times larger than life.

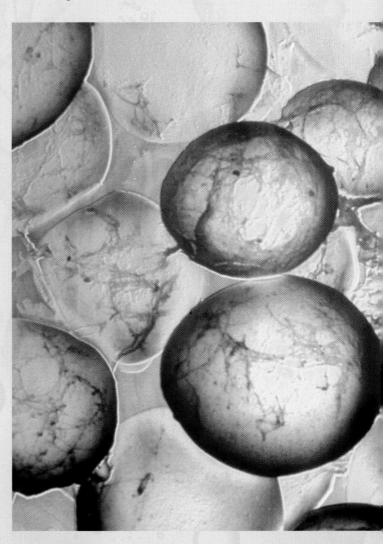

7

INSIDE A CELL

Cells are tiny 'building block' units that make up all living things. But although cells are small, they are not simple. Each cell has many different parts inside, including a control centre which contains the genes.

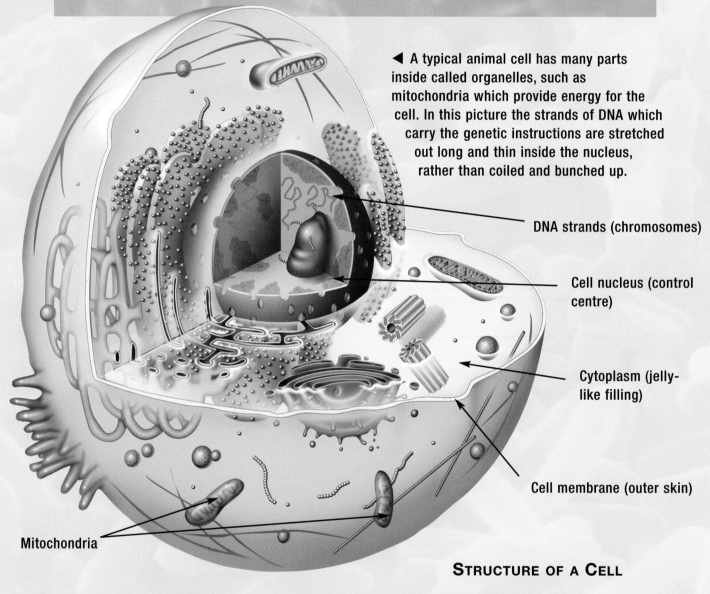

◄ A typical animal cell has many parts inside called organelles, such as mitochondria which provide energy for the cell. In this picture the strands of DNA which carry the genetic instructions are stretched out long and thin inside the nucleus, rather than coiled and bunched up.

DNA strands (chromosomes)

Cell nucleus (control centre)

Cytoplasm (jelly-like filling)

Cell membrane (outer skin)

Mitochondria

STRUCTURE OF A CELL

CELL PARTS

There are many different types of cells, but most have the same basic parts. A cell is surrounded by a protective skin called the cell membrane, which holds all its parts together.

Inside is a watery jelly, cytoplasm. Floating in the cytoplasm are smaller parts known as organelles, which do different jobs for the cell. The cell also has a 'headquarters' or control centre – the nucleus. This contains the genes.

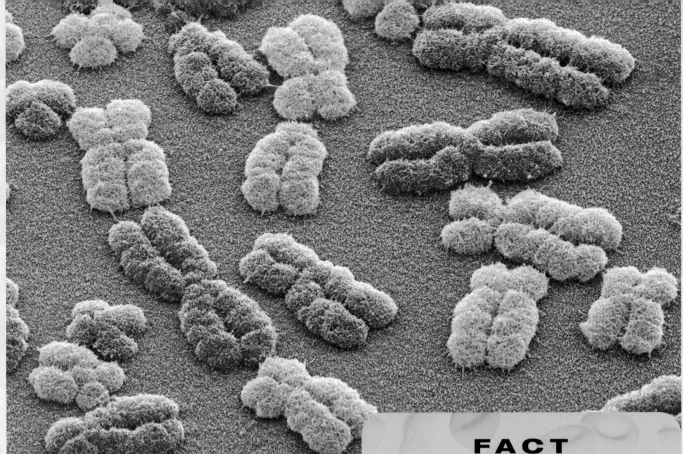

▲ Chromosomes are lengths or strands of DNA inside a cell's nucleus. In this computer-coloured photograph each chromosome is coiled into a much shorter and thicker shape, like an X.

CHROMOSOMES

The genes are in the form of long strands of the chemical DNA. Each strand is called a chromosome. A typical cell in the human body contains 46 separate strands of DNA – that is, 46 chromosomes. All together, the 46 chromosomes in each cell contain the complete set of human genes.

Other kinds of living things have different numbers of chromosomes in their cells. For example a housefly has 12 in each cell, a dog has 78, a sweet potato plant has 90 and a goldfish has 94. The number of chromosomes in each cell is not linked to how complicated a living thing is, or its size.

SHAPES OF CHROMOSOMES

The strand of DNA which makes up one chromosome is usually very long and thin, like a length of unwound, stretched-out string. It is difficult to see through an ordinary microscope. But at certain times, for example, when the cell is about to divide, the strand

coils and bunches itself into a much shorter, thicker shape, more like a ball of string. This makes it much easier to see the chromosome through a microscope. Photographs of chromosomes taken using a microscope usually show them in this bunched-up form, as X-like shapes.

GENE SECTIONS

A single gene is one small part or section of DNA along the whole strand or chromosome. In a human cell, a typical chromosome has more than 1,000 genes along it.

ALL ABOUT DNA

The instructions or genes for living things are made of DNA. But what is DNA? It's a type of chemical, made up of smaller chemical units joined together into a long strand or string. The letters DNA stand for the chemical's full name, deoxyribonucleic acid.

SHAPE OF DNA

All objects, substances and materials throughout the Universe are made of tiny particles of matter, called atoms. DNA is made of atoms. In fact each piece of DNA is made of millions of atoms. These join together to form one long, thin length or strand of DNA – a chromosome. Because of the way that the atoms fit together, DNA has a coiled shape. It is similar to a ladder which has been twisted like a corkscrew. This shape is known as the DNA double helix.

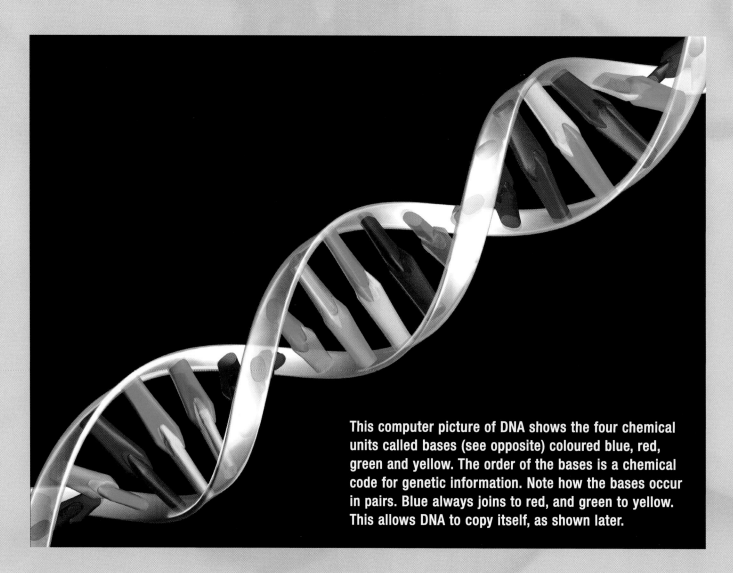

This computer picture of DNA shows the four chemical units called bases (see opposite) coloured blue, red, green and yellow. The order of the bases is a chemical code for genetic information. Note how the bases occur in pairs. Blue always joins to red, and green to yellow. This allows DNA to copy itself, as shown later.

▲ A scientist holds up DNA taken out of a tomato plant. Each of the tiny pale 'strings' in the clump contains millions of individual strands of DNA.

SEEING DNA

A single stretched-out strand of DNA is very long, but it is so narrow that it is difficult to see, even with the most powerful microscope. However, when millions of DNA strands clump together, we can see them even without a microscope. They look like stringy white gloop. Scientists can take out, or extract, DNA as lumps like this from any living thing. The DNA can then be studied and tested.

FOUR BASES

The length or strand of DNA contains smaller chemical units known as bases. There are four bases in DNA: adenine, cytosine, guanine and thymine. They are usually known by their first letters as A, C, G and T. Along a single strand of DNA (a chromosome) there are many millions of these bases.

IMPORTANT ORDER

A gene is one section of DNA, with its own particular sequence of As, Cs, Gs and Ts. This pattern or order of the bases is very important. The bases are a code, in a chemical form, that 'spells' the instructions of the gene. The cell knows what to do because it can read the code. It's like a cook reading a recipe, choosing the ingredients and following the instructions.

HOW GENES WORK

Microscopic cells produce the substances needed to make a living thing work – including the materials needed to make new cells. Genes work by telling each cell how to produce certain substances.

THE FULL SET OF GENES

Each cell in a living thing contains all of the genes needed for that living thing. For example, a fruit fly has about 13,600 genes. Each of the fruit fly's cells contains all of these genes, in the form of strands of DNA. Scientists think that a human body has about 30,000 genes. So every human body cell has the whole set of 30,000 genes.

A cell makes a particular body substance or product using instructions in the gene for that substance. For example, our hairs grow from tiny pockets in the skin called hair follicles. Inside each hair follicle, thousands of cells make the substance known as keratin. This is tough and hard, and builds into a long, thin rod – a hair. Each hair-making follicle cell follows the instructions in the gene for making keratin, which is known as the keratin gene.

◀ A human hair gets longer by about 0.35mm per day, as thousands of cells use the instructions in their keratin genes to make the tough, hard substance keratin.

FACT FOCUS

FOOD FOR CELLS

When a cell makes a body substance like keratin, it needs lots of different chemical ingredients. These come from food. Healthy foods contain plenty of different chemical ingredients, and help the body to work better. For example, a chemical ingredient called lysine is important for building healthy hair. It is found in fish, milk, beans, cheese, meat and eggs.

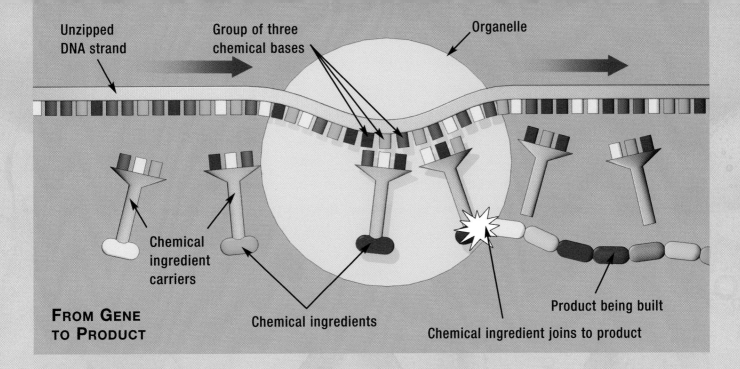

Unzipped DNA strand

Group of three chemical bases

Organelle

Chemical ingredient carriers

Chemical ingredients

Chemical ingredient joins to product

Product being built

FROM GENE TO PRODUCT

READING THE CODE

The instructions in a gene are written in a 'code' using the four chemical units in DNA called bases, as shown previously. To read the code, first the strand or double helix of DNA comes apart down the middle, like a zip. Then one of the cell's organelles (tiny parts) moves along one of the half-strands of the DNA. For each group of three bases on the DNA, the organelle chooses a particular chemical ingredient and sticks it to a previous one. One by one the chemical ingredients gradually build up into the required substance or product. So, for example, the keratin gene tells the cell which chemical ingredients to stick together, and in which order, to make keratin for a hair.

BUILDING BODY PARTS

By reading the coded instructions in genes, cells can make whatever the body needs. The genes used by a particular cell depend on the cell's position in the body, which cells are around it, and the amounts of various controlling substances in and around the cell, including substances called growth factors.

Different types of cells are always at work all over the body, reading various genes and making the different substances that the body needs. The cells renew hair, skin and nails. They replace wear and tear in muscles and bones. They make the digestive chemicals needed to break apart food, and they do all the other jobs needed to keep the body alive.

▲ To read genetic instructions, the DNA strand 'unzips'. An organelle moves along one half and reads the code of each group of three bases. It selects the chemical ingredient for that code, and joins these chemical ingredients together to make the product.

▼ In every living thing, from a flower to a leopard, cells are busy reading genes and making body substances – even during sleep.

MAKING NEW CELLS

Cells make new cells by splitting in two. This is always happening in every living thing. It is part of normal growth, and it is how body parts are maintained and repaired after damage.

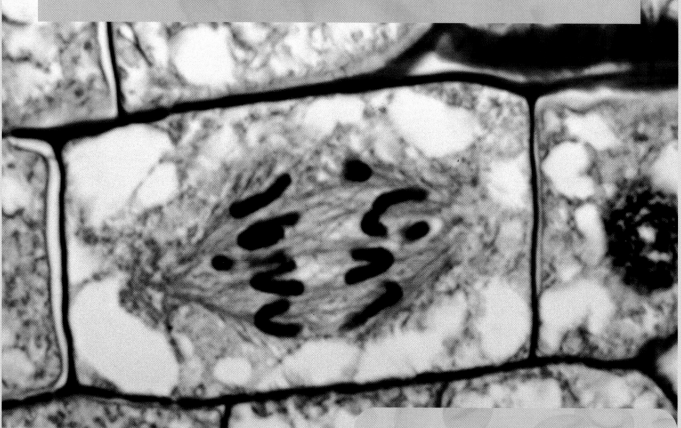

▲ This box-shaped cell from an onion plant has copied all of its DNA to make a new set of chromosomes. One set is now moving to each end of the cell, before the cell itself splits in two.

CELL DIVISION

To split or divide, first a cell grows bigger. It builds extra organelles and other cell materials inside, so that there is enough to share between the two cells which will result. The cell's nucleus splits in two, so there are two control centres. This splitting process is called mitosis. Then the whole cell divides into two as well. Finally the two halves become two new cells, with one nucleus in each.

EVIDENCE FOCUS

AMAZING REPAIR
You can see the results of cell division if you have a skin injury like a cut. First the blood clots to form a sticky lump, which hardens into a protective scab. Under this, skin cells start to divide at incredible speed. They make new skin cells so that the cut edges of skin gradually grow towards each other, while more new cells grow up from beneath. After just a few days, billions of new skin cells have healed the cut.

COPYING GENES

When a cell divides to make two new cells, it cannot share out its genes between them. Otherwise each resulting cell would not have a complete set. Instead the cell copies all of its genes – that is, makes a new set of chromosomes – so that each new cell will have the full set. This copying happens before mitosis. When the nucleus splits, the two sets of chromosomes separate, with one set going into each new nucleus.

DNA DOUBLING

DNA's design makes it easy to copy itself. First the strand or double helix unzips along the middle, to form two half-strands. Then each half-strand rebuilds its missing side. It can do this accurately because of the way the bases (chemical units) link in pairs, as shown earlier. A always links to T, and C to G. So the chemical units of the newly built half-strand have to join together in exactly the same order as in the old half-strand.

The result is two DNA strands that are exact copies of the original – and of each other. This copying process is called DNA replication.

FAST DIVISION

New cells are made in a living thing like the human body at an amazing rate. Every second about five million of your cells, having copied all their genes, divide into two. This makes 10 million new cells to replace those which wear out and die, as part of natural body maintenance.

▶ A double helix of DNA (at the top of this picture) copies or replicates itself by coming apart along the middle into two half-strands. Then each of these half-strands builds a new partner which is the same as its previous one. This forms two identical strands (shown at the bottom).

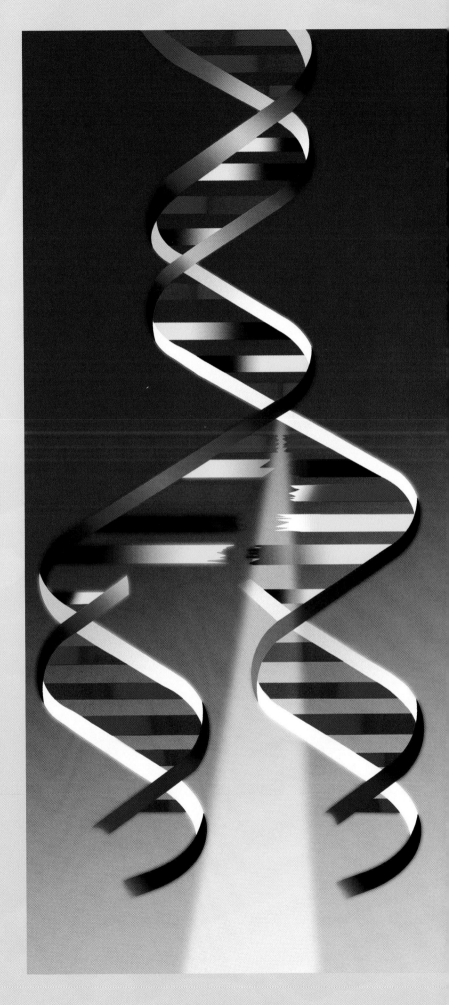

PASSING ON GENES

When living things breed or reproduce, they pass on their genes to their offspring (young). The offspring then grow up to look like their parents, as members of the same species.

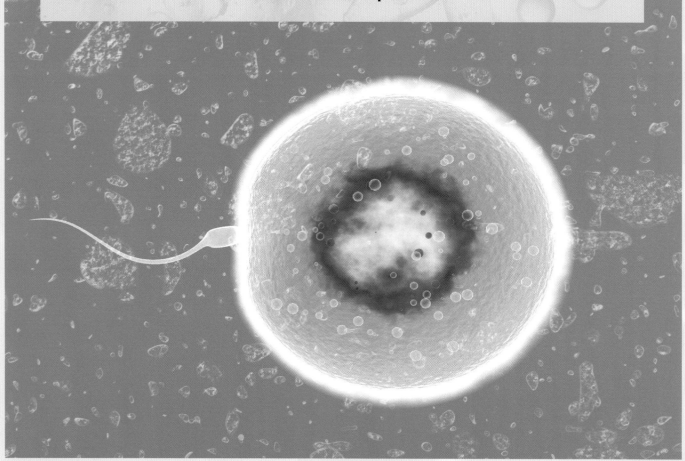

TWO CELLS

Most living things, including humans, cats, dogs, pandas, butterflies and flowering plants, reproduce by combining two reproductive cells, one male and one female. For example, when a male and female giant panda mate, a male sperm cell fuses with a female egg cell inside the female panda's body. This makes a new cell called a fertilised egg that grows into a baby panda.

If two normal cells joined to make a fertilised egg, each with the full set of chromosomes, the fertilised egg would have twice the usual number

▲ Egg cells from a female animal are large and round. Sperm cells from a male are smaller and tadpole-shaped. When an egg joins a sperm to start a new living thing, this is called fertilisation.

of chromosomes. But this would mean the cell could not work properly. So reproductive cells are formed by a different kind of cell division. As egg and sperm cells form, they receive only half the number of chromosomes, by a type of division called meiosis. Then, when an egg and sperm join, the fertilised egg has the normal number of chromosomes again.

A NEW SET OF GENES

In humans, a normal cell has 46 chromosomes. These are in 23 pairs. Each human reproductive cell – egg or sperm – has only one of each pair, numbering 23 chromosomes. When an egg and sperm join, the fertilised egg has 46 chromosomes again, as 23 pairs. This means a baby has a selection of genes from both its parents. So it does not grow up as an exact copy of either parent. It is a new individual, with a unique combination of genes.

EXACT COPIES

Some living things can make babies in another way, with just one parent. The tiny water creature called the hydra reproduces by 'budding'. It grows a kind of branch called a bud, which breaks off and enlarges into a new hydra. This offspring is made of cells from the parent and has the same genes as the parent (see page 32).

▶ A baby receives genes from both its mother and its father. This baby orang-utan will have a combination of features, some similar to one parent and some more like the other parent.

▼ This tiny water creature, a hydra, is growing two side 'buds' (pointing to the upper and lower right) on its long stalk. Each bud will become a new hydra, with exactly the same genes as the parent.

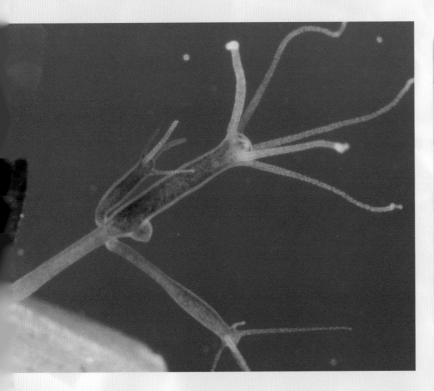

FACT FOCUS

IDENTICAL TWINS
Most children get a unique, one-off combination of genes from both their parents. Even in the same family, brothers and sisters have slightly different combinations of their parents' genes, so they look different from each other. The only people who have exactly the same genes as each other are identical twins. They begin when a single fertilised egg cell splits into two cells, each with the same genes. Then these two cells separate and each grows into a baby (see page 21).

BABY
BLUEPRINT

As well as containing instructions for how to make body substances, genes control the way a living thing grows and develops. All the genetic instructions needed to build an adult living thing are there from its beginning, when it was just one cell, the fertilised egg.

EARLY DEVELOPMENT

An animal like a tortoise begins life as a fertilised egg cell made from two reproductive cells, the egg and sperm, from its parents. The fertilised egg cell contains a complete set of tortoise genes that will tell it how to grow and develop inside its egg, into a baby tortoise.

The first genetic instruction that the fertilised egg cell carries out is to divide or split into two

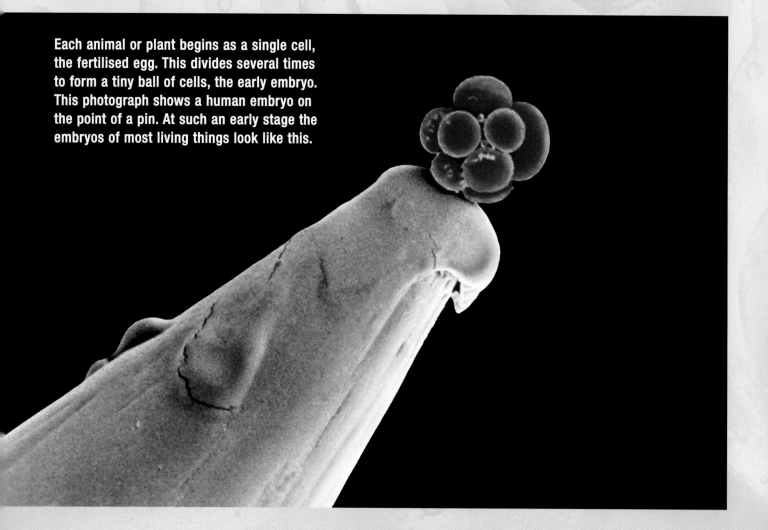

Each animal or plant begins as a single cell, the fertilised egg. This divides several times to form a tiny ball of cells, the early embryo. This photograph shows a human embryo on the point of a pin. At such an early stage the embryos of most living things look like this.

▶ After much growing and developing, an embryo becomes a baby plant or animal – like this tortoise. The genes are still working after this time, giving instructions on how to grow into an adult.

cells. Each of these cells splits again, making four cells. This cell division carries on to form a small ball of cells, then a larger one. These cells have been formed by the division called mitosis, and so each has a complete set of genes. This early stage in the development of a living thing is called an embryo.

CELL CHANGES

After the embryo has been growing for a few days, genes tell the cells to start changing into different types of cells. In a baby animal some will become brain cells, some muscle cells, some bone cells and so on. The genes also tell these different cells how to group together, move about and form body parts. In the tortoise, different sets of cells form its outer shell, its scaly skin, its four clawed legs, its beady eyes and many other parts. The same happens in other kinds of animals and plants, as the embryo follows its genetic instructions and grows into a member of its species.

GROWING UP

Finally the baby tortoise is ready to hatch out of its egg. Many other animals hatch from eggs, such as worms, spiders, crocodiles and

birds. In mammals, the embryo develops in its mother's body and emerges as a newborn baby. But all baby animals still have a lot of growing to do. So do plants, which grow from tiny seeds. This growth is partly under the control of genetic instructions, but is also affected by the surroundings (see page 26).

FACT FOCUS

HOW A HUMAN GROWS

A human baby, like most kinds of animals and plants, grows from a fertilised egg cell. By the time the human baby is ready to be born nine months later, that one cell has divided many times to become more than 200 billion cells. After being born, humans take longer than almost any other animal species to become adults – up to 20 years. This growth and development, from baby to child to adult, is partly under the control of genetic instructions.

GENETIC TRAITS

Genetic traits are features that get passed on from parents to offspring, in the genes. Hair colour, eye colour, skin colour, and the shape of a person's nose, earlobes and other body parts, are all examples of human genetic traits.

ALIKE BUT DIFFERENT

All the members of a species – such as humans, pandas, cats or pea plants – look roughly the same and behave in a similar way. For example, all domestic cats have four legs, long swishy tails and sharp teeth and claws. They like meaty food, and lick themselves clean.

But domestic cats are not all exactly the same. They come in different sizes and have different colours and patterns in their fur. It's the same with humans. It is easy to tell apart people from animals by their general body shape and behaviour. But humans do not all look exactly the same as each other. They come in many different shapes and sizes, with different skin, hair and eye colours. These small differences between individuals of one kind or species are known as genetic traits.

◄ These baby kittens came from the same mother and father. But each kitten received a slightly different combination of cat genes. So the kittens look and behave differently.

◄ These two children are identical twins. Even though they have the same genes, they will grow up to look slightly different. This shows the effect of the conditions around us as we grow, as well as the genetic instructions inside us (see page 26).

INHERITING TRAITS

When children inherit their genes from their parents, they get one version or allele from each parent. These alleles come together in different combinations for each offspring. So one child might have eyes similar to its mother's and a nose shape similar to its father's – while another child in the same family has the reverse. However the different versions or alleles can work together in complicated ways, as shown on the next page.

WHAT CAUSES TRAITS?

Genetic traits happen because even in the same species, there are slight differences between the genes of individuals. For example, all humans have genes for making hair. But instead of just one version of the hair gene, there are several different versions. They all do the same job, but they do it slightly differently. The different versions make different types of hair, ranging from black to light, and from straight to curly or frizzy. Different versions of the same gene are called alleles.

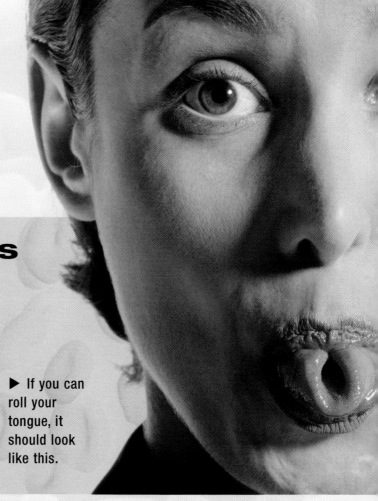

▶ If you can roll your tongue, it should look like this.

EVIDENCE FOCUS

TONGUE-ROLLING

The ability to roll the tongue into a U-shape or tube is a genetic trait. Some people can do it because they have a certain version of the tongue-rolling gene, while others have a different version of the gene and cannot. Try it yourself. You could also test whether your family members, friends and people at school can do it. Do children who can roll their tongues have parents who can do this too?

TYPES OF TRAITS

Some types of genetic traits are 'stronger', and more likely to affect a living thing, than others. These 'stronger' traits are called dominant traits, while 'weaker' ones are recessive traits.

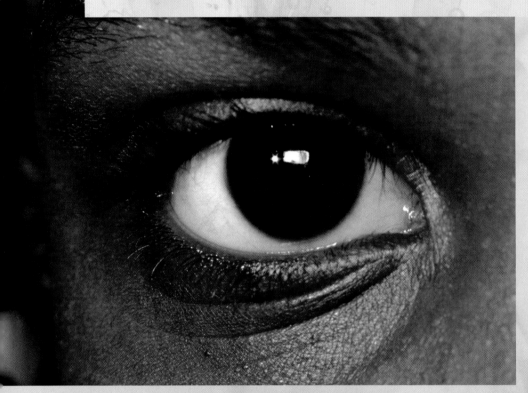

▲ Eye colour is the result of different versions, or alleles, of the same gene. One allele comes from each parent. The brown allele for eye colour causes the iris part of the eye to be brown.

TWO OF EACH

As explained earlier, chromosomes are usually found in pairs inside a cell. For example, humans have 46 chromosomes in each cell, made up of 23 pairs. The two chromosomes in a pair have the same genes on them, like the gene for eye colour, the gene for ear shape, the gene for skin colour, and so on. So a living thing such as a human actually has two versions of each gene, called alleles. One version came from each parent.

Sometimes the two alleles are the same. Then it does not matter which one is used, since they both give the same result. But sometimes there are two different alleles of a gene. What happens then?

WHICH IS STRONGER?

If a living thing has two different alleles of a gene, it usually uses only one of them – the dominant or stronger one. For example, with the gene for eye colour in humans, the allele for brown eyes is stronger or dominant. The allele for blue eyes is weaker or recessive. If a person has one brown allele and one blue allele, the brown one is dominant and the person has brown eyes. Having brown eyes is known as a dominant trait.

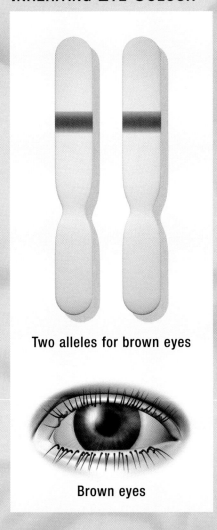

Two alleles for brown eyes

Brown eyes

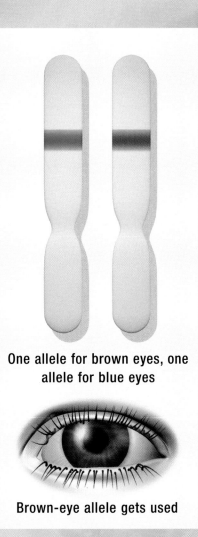

One allele for brown eyes, one allele for blue eyes

Brown-eye allele gets used

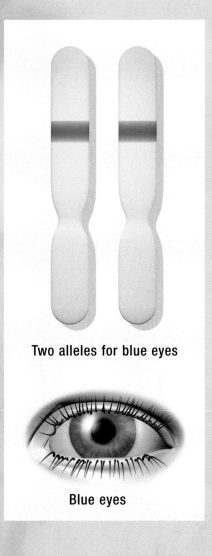

Two alleles for blue eyes

Blue eyes

▲ Here is the pair of chromosomes which carry the eye colour gene. One allele came from each parent. If a person has two brown alleles, their eyes are brown. One brown allele and one blue allele still produce brown eyes, because brown is dominant. Two blue alleles give blue eyes.

THE POWER OF TWO

Recessive alleles, such as the allele for blue eyes, can still get used if there is no dominant allele to rule them out. If a person has two alleles for blue eyes, he or she will have blue eyes. So having blue eyes is known as a recessive trait.

Everyone gets a unique combination of alleles, one of each pair from each parent. Due to dominant and recessive traits, it's possible for a person to have a different eye colour from their parents. The same applies to other genetic traits like hair colour, earlobe shape, skin colour and the shape of the nose.

EVIDENCE FOCUS

EARLOBE EXPERIMENT

Check your earlobes in a mirror. Do they have a flap that hangs down at the bottom edge, called a hanging earlobe? Or do they have a straight bottom edge, called an attached earlobe?

- Hanging earlobes is the dominant trait. So if you have hanging earlobes, then of your two alleles for earlobe shape, one or both are for hanging earlobes.

- Attached earlobes is a recessive trait. If you have these, you must have two alleles for attached earlobes.

GENETIC DISEASES

Some diseases are caused by genes which are missing or not working properly. Because genes are passed on from parents to children, that means diseases can be passed on too. These are known as inherited or genetic conditions.

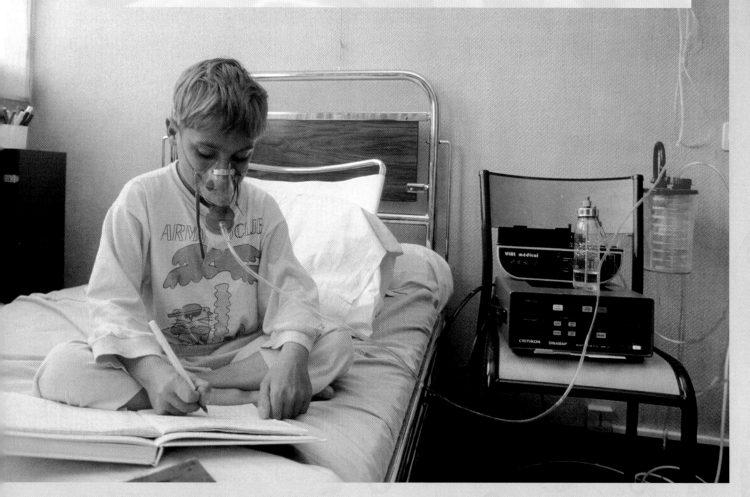

PROBLEM GENES

There are hundreds of different types of inherited conditions, usually caused by a problem with a particular gene or a whole chromosome. For example, cystic fibrosis is caused by a fault in a particular gene. If this gene is working well, it tells cells how to make a substance that helps the lungs and several other body parts to work properly. The faulty version of the gene does not do this. The cells

▲ This boy has cystic fibrosis, which makes breathing difficult. He is using a machine called a nebuliser to help him breathe.

cannot make the substance, and the lungs do not work properly, making it hard to breathe.

RECESSIVE DISEASES

Inherited conditions often involve dominant and recessive alleles (as explained on the previous pages). Many inherited diseases, including cystic fibrosis, are recessive. If a person has one healthy version or allele of the gene and one faulty version, and the healthy one is dominant, there is no problem. Only if a person receives two faulty versions, one from each parent, will the condition develop.

CARRIERS

If a person has a faulty version of a gene, but does not have the condition it causes, this is called being a carrier. Often a carrier has one healthy allele which is dominant, and one recessive allele which is faulty. The dominant one overpowers the recessive one.

A carrier may pass the condition to her or his children, depending on which allele is inherited by each child. For example, if two carrier parents both pass on the faulty allele to their child, that child will have the condition. This means inherited diseases run in families, but not everyone in the family gets them. Sometimes a condition can 'skip a generation'. This means it could show up in grandparents and grandchildren, but not in the parents, who are themselves carriers.

HIGHER CHANCES

Some faulty versions of genes do not cause diseases, but they do make problems more likely. For example, some families have a combination of genes that make them more likely to get a certain type of cancer, such as bowel cancer. This may be because they lack the versions of the genes that fight off the disease, rather than because they have genes which cause it.

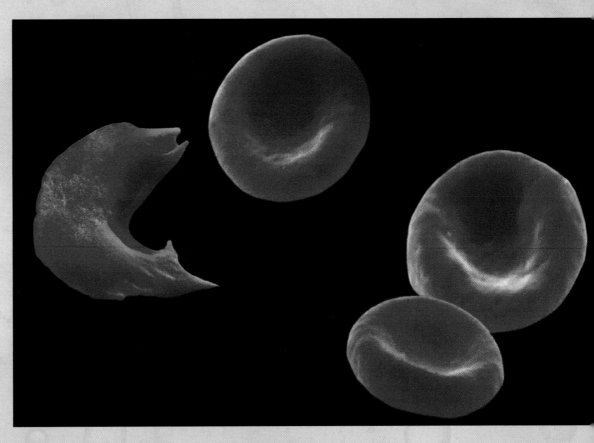

▶ In the inherited condition known as sickle-cell disorder, some of the oxygen-carrying red cells in the blood become curved or 'sickled', like the one shown here on the left. They cannot work well and they block blood vessels, causing pain and other problems. Sickle-cell disorder is one of dozens of inherited conditions affecting the blood.

NATURE AND NURTURE

Genes decide much about a living thing before it is even born – from its species to its body shape, appearance and sometimes even the diseases it will get. But genes are not the whole story.

► Being good at a sport is a mixture of nature and nurture. Nature (genes) can make someone strong, with fast reactions and good stamina. But nurture is also essential – learning how to play, practising regularly and eating healthily.

FACT FOCUS

FOODS FOR LOOKS AND HEALTH
Some foods have an effect on the way you look and how healthy you are. They are a 'nurture' way of helping to improve 'nature', that is, genes. Here are a few:

• Fish, meat, beans and yogurt contain protein, which helps to build healthy hair, muscles, skin and bones.

• B vitamins help to keep skin strong and supple. They are found in meat, potatoes, bread and milk.

• Iron, found in red meat, eggs and leafy vegetables, helps keep fingernails strong and blood healthy.

• Oily fish like salmon, mackerel and tuna are good for the heart, and may also help children do better at school.

BITS OF BOTH
Genes are important in deciding what a living thing will be like. A person's adult height, appearance, health, and some abilities like athletic skills, are all influenced by genes – before that person is even born. But there are many other influences too. They include the person's family life, experiences at school, food, friends and the general way that the person is brought up.

These two different kinds of influences are often called 'nature' and 'nurture'. 'Nature' means the genes a person is born with. This happens for natural reasons and is very hard to change. 'Nurture' means the way that surroundings and experiences influence the person, which often can be altered. Many experts argue about which is more important, 'nature' or 'nurture'.

LEARNING

Whatever genes a person has, that person needs to learn while growing up. For example, children learn to talk by listening to people around them speaking. Genes have some effects on how clever or intelligent a person is, but education has great effects too. Children who start learning about letters and numbers early, while they are toddlers, often make faster progress when they go to school.

HEALTH AND DIET

Genes affect a person's basic body shape and appearance, like being tall or short. But people can also influence these features by 'nurture' – the way they live. If a child has a very healthy diet from birth, it may grow faster and end up taller than it would with a less healthy diet. Eating a combination of healthy foods can improve hair and skin. 'Nurture' effects such as air pollution and amount of sunlight can affect health badly. How much a person eats or exercises has a great effect on body weight.

Overall, people can use 'nurture' to make many changes to the features that 'nature' has given them in the form of genes. Geneticists (gene scientists) are also finding ways to change the genes themselves, as shown on later pages.

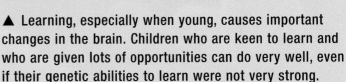

▲ Learning, especially when young, causes important changes in the brain. Children who are keen to learn and who are given lots of opportunities can do very well, even if their genetic abilities to learn were not very strong.

▼ A sheepdog shows how nature and nurture combine. Sheepdogs are bred for their intelligence and obedience, which is partly in their genes. But they also have to learn how to round up sheep and understand their trainer's signals.

DISCOVERING GENES

Genes were not discovered by one single person. It took many scientists many years to piece together the evidence and find out about genes, chromosomes and DNA. This exciting work continues today.

▲ Over several years Gregor Mendel studied pea plants in his monastery garden. He grew more than 28,000 of them. His work was ignored during his lifetime, but today Mendel is regarded as the founder of genetics.

PLENTY OF PEAS

Gregor Mendel was the first real gene scientist or geneticist. He was an Austrian monk who was interested in living things, and did experiments on pea plants in his monastery garden in the 1860s. Mendel studied the way pea plants inherited various features, such as plant height, flower colour and pea shape. (Today we would call these features genetic traits.) He also discovered how some versions of genes were dominant and others were recessive.

PROVED RIGHT

Mendel could not see genes, as strands of DNA. The microscopes of his time were not powerful enough. Neither did he call them 'genes' since this word had not been invented. He called them 'hereditary factors'. But his experiments did prove that what we call genes existed. When he tried to announce this, however, most scientists ignored him. It was only around 1890, long after he died, that scientists using better microscopes saw DNA as chromosomes inside cells. They repeated Mendel's experiments and realised that he had been right.

THE TALE OF DNA

By the late 1940s, scientists had found out that each human cell contained 23 pairs of chromosomes, and that chromosomes contained genes and were made of DNA.

However, they did not yet have enough information to know how DNA worked.

In 1951 a scientist named Rosalind Franklin used a kind of X-ray photograph to find out what DNA looked like. Her photos showed that it had a helix or corkscrew-like shape.

A MOMENTOUS DISCOVERY

Rosalind Franklin's co-worker Maurice Wilkins passed her results to two other scientists, James Watson and Francis Crick. In 1953 they worked out the detailed double helix structure of DNA. They showed how the four chemical units called bases fit together along a DNA strand, and how this allows DNA to copy itself. It was one of the most important advances in all of science.

▶ James Watson (left) and Francis Crick worked out the shape of DNA as a double helix. They used balls and sticks to make different models of DNA until they decided on the correct one.

▶ One of Rosalind Franklin's X-ray photographs of the crystalline form of DNA.

HISTORY FOCUS

MISSED OUT

Rosalind Franklin took many photographs of DNA which helped Watson and Crick to work out its shape. The photos were taken using X-rays and did not show the shape directly, but as patterns of stripes and spots that needed careful study. In 1962 Watson and Crick, together with Wilkins, were awarded the Nobel Prize for their work on DNA. Sadly Franklin, who had died four years earlier, was not included in the honour.

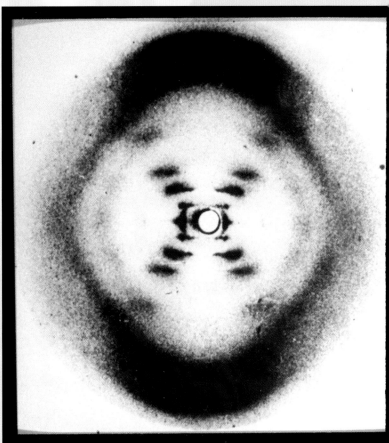

GENETIC ENGINEERING

Genetic engineering, or GE, is also called genetic modification, or GM. It means changing the DNA of living things. Genes are added, taken away or altered. This makes plants, animals, microbes and even humans grow and work differently.

1 A chromosome is removed from the cell of a living thing, and a gene taken out as a length of DNA.

4 The fertilised egg cell develops into a new living thing, and all of its cells carry copies of the extra gene.

GENE TRANSFER
This is one method of taking a gene from one living thing and adding it to another.

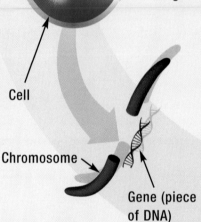

Cell

Chromosome

Gene (piece of DNA)

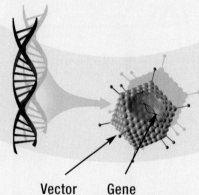

Vector   Gene

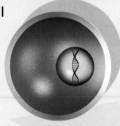

Nucleus of fertilised egg cell

2 The DNA is put into a 'carrier' or vector, in this case, a microbe called a virus.

3 The vector is put into a fertilised egg cell, which is ready to grow. The vector adds the extra gene into the egg cell's DNA.

MOVING GENES

A living thing's genes tell it how to make body substances and build body parts. So, by changing its genes, or adding a new gene, scientists can make a living thing grow in a different way. Or they can make it produce a substance that it would not normally make.

For example, genetic engineering has been used to add a gene from a spider, which instructs how to make spider silk, to the cells of a goat. The goat's cells then follow the instructions in the gene, and make tiny strands of spider silk. These can be collected from the goat's milk and woven together to make thread. This was an experiment to try and produce new types of strong cloth. Genetically engineered animals and plants like this are new types of living things that cannot occur in nature. The new combinations of DNA, with genes from different living things added together, are called recombinant DNA.

GM CROPS

Genetic engineering has been used to change the genes of plants to try to make better farm crops. These are usually known as GM crops. For example:

- GM strawberries have a gene from a flounder fish added to them. The fish gene makes a substance that stops the strawberries from freezing and becoming spoiled if they get very cold.

- GM cotton plants have extra genes to make a poisonous substance that kills some types of insect pests.

- GM soybeans have been altered to resist a certain weedkiller. This means farmers can use the weedkiller on their fields to banish weeds without harming the crop.

BIG BUSINESS

Scientists work on genetic engineering partly to find out more about genes. They also do it because GM animals and crops might make a lot of money. Many big businesses pay gene scientists to work for them, designing genetically engineered crops and other genetic inventions. This is one reason why the science of genetics moves so fast – there is plenty of money involved.

▲ Scientists must carry out genetic experiments very carefully. For example, GM crops are first grown in greenhouses, where pests and diseases are less likely to affect them and ruin the test results.

FACT FOCUS

GM CROPS

More than two-thirds of the world's GM crops are grown in the USA, followed by Canada, Argentina and China. Ten other countries grow much smaller amounts. In the early twenty-first century GM crops were grown on more than 60 million hectares worldwide – more than twice the area of the UK. The four main GM crops were soy (soya or soybean) with 37 million hectares, corn (maize) with 12 million, cotton at 7 million, and canola (oil-seed rape) at 4 million hectares.

CLONING AND CHOOSING

Gene science can change the way living things are made. This may mean choosing embryos at a very early stage of development for certain genetic features, or making exact genetic copies, called clones.

CLONING

Clones are living things which have the same genes as each other. Clones occur in nature. For example, a hydra's offspring made by budding have the same genes as their one parent (see page 17). So are young plants which grow as runners from a parent plant. But geneticists have also found ways of cloning animals such as sheep, cows, cats and dogs, in which cloning does not happen in nature.

WHY CLONE?

The scientific process of cloning works by taking a set of genes from an adult cell, and putting them into an egg cell which has had its

▼ In cloning, the DNA in a fertilised egg cell is taken out, and the DNA from another living thing is put in. The egg is held steady on a narrow blunt-pointed pipette (below left). The new DNA is injected using a very sharp-pointed glass needle.

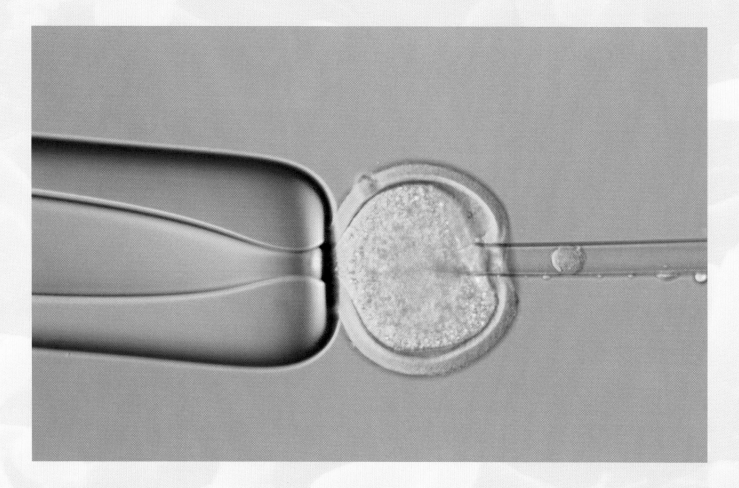

▲ Cloned pigs are part of research to see if pig organs, like the heart or liver, could be transplanted into people. If one pig's genes can be altered so that human patients are less likely to reject its organs, then clones of this pig could be 'living organ banks'.

own genes taken out. The egg cell uses the new genes to develop and grow. Cloning could be used to 'copy' chickens that lay the most eggs and cows that produce the most milk. But at present this type of cloning is costly, not very reliable and still mainly experimental.

SELECTING GENES

Choosing human eggs, sperm or embryos can help people who risk passing on an inherited disease to their offspring. The eggs, sperm or tiny embryos are tested for genetic problems, and only healthy ones are used. This can be done when eggs and sperm join in a laboratory container, which is called IVF (*in vitro* fertilisation). After testing, the healthy embryo is put into the mother's womb to grow and develop as usual.

'DESIGNER BABIES'

The phrase 'designer baby' means a baby which grows from an embryo selected for its particular genes – usually to make sure it is healthy. So far, scientists do not actually 'design' human babies by choosing features like hair colour, body height, intelligence or whether a baby is a boy or girl. But this might happen in the future.

SPEED OF PROGRESS

The science of genetics is moving ahead fast. It makes possible procedures which most people have never dreamed of. As research forges ahead, existing laws and regulations become out of date. Genetics poses questions that society in general must consider, as we decide what we do and do not want (see page 38).

GENETIC MEDICINE

Now that scientists know how some inherited diseases work, they are searching for genetic medicines to treat them. Gene science can help to treat other kinds of illness too.

▲ In this factory, huge vats called fermentation units contain bacteria which have been genetically engineered to make a particular substance, in this case a medical drug.

MAKING MEDICINES

In some illnesses the body cannot make certain natural substances which it needs to work properly. In an illness like this, if scientists can find the gene for making this natural substance, they can use it to make the substance outside the body, then put the substance into the body.

PRODUCING INSULIN

Insulin is a hormone – a natural substance found in the body – which controls the amount of sugar in the blood. People with the condition called diabetes cannot produce enough insulin, so they may have to inject it. To make insulin supplies, scientists have inserted human insulin genes into a type of bacteria called *E. coli*. The bacteria follow the

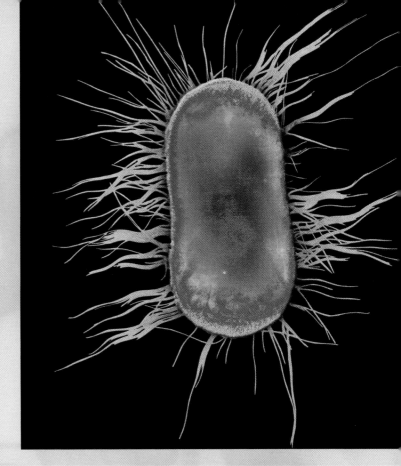

▶ *Escherichia coli*, often called *E. coli*, is a type of bacterium that can have its genes altered to make various medicines, including antibiotics and hormones. It is shown here about 20,000 times larger than life.

instructions in the insulin genes and make insulin, which is then collected and purified for people with diabetes.

CRACKING CANCER

Cancers are a range of serious, sometimes deadly diseases. We still do not know exactly how some forms of cancer develop. But scientists have found that if the DNA in body cells is damaged, this makes certain cancers more likely. Some people also have genes that seem to protect them against cancers. So scientists are working on ways to cure cancer by repairing faulty genes, and to prevent cancer by giving people anti-cancer genes.

GENE THERAPY

Some genetic diseases happen because certain genes are missing or do not work. Gene therapy is a treatment that inserts healthy genes into a person's body. It often uses microbes such as bacteria or viruses as vectors to carry the new genes into body cells (see page 30). Progress with gene therapy has been slow, but it has had some success in treating conditions such as cystic fibrosis.

▼ Covering up in the sun, and using sunscreen creams or sprays, help to filter out the sun's UV (ultra-violet) rays. These rays can alter DNA in skin cells and lead to various forms of skin cancer.

FACT FOCUS

DNA DAMAGE
Some types of cancer are caused by damage to the DNA inside cells. One major cause of such damage is smoking. It not only harms cells in the lungs and leads to lung cancer, but it also makes other types of cancers more likely in other parts of the body. Everyone can reduce the chance of developing cancer, simply by not smoking.

DNA MAPPING AND TESTING

Modern genetic equipment allows scientists to take samples of DNA and read the chemical codes in them. This means they can test people's DNA, and make 'maps' of the DNA in living things.

MAPPING GENOMES

A genome is the complete set of all the genes and DNA that a living thing has in its cells. This genetic information is carried as the order or sequence of the chemical bases A, C, G and

▼ A scientist studies a computer display of DNA sequences, which shows the order of the chemical bases along a strand of DNA. The sequences are in the form of patterns of black stripes, which look similar to a supermarket bar code.

T along the strands of DNA. Scientists can read this sequence and so 'map' the genomes of living things. Then, from the order of the bases, scientists can work out which genes are where along the different strands, or chromosomes, of DNA (see page 9).

This job is complex and time-consuming. DNA samples must be cut into short sections using different chemicals, and put through a DNA sequencing machine. This makes the sections

of DNA move through a special clear gel, which sorts them into groups. Computers then work out which chemical bases are where.

GENOMES SO FAR
The first living things to have their genomes mapped – that is, the order of the bases worked out – include:

- *E. coli* bacteria in 1997

- a tiny roundworm (the nematode *Caenorhabditis*) in 1998

- the fruit fly (*Drosophila*) in 2000

- the mouse in 2001

- the rice plant in 2002

- the human being in 2003.

DNA TESTING
Everyone has a unique pattern of fingerprints – and of DNA. So DNA 'fingerprinting' can be used to identify a person. For example, at a crime scene tiny traces of skin cells, saliva (spit), blood or hairs can be tested for their DNA patterns. The results are matched against

▲ The fruit fly *Drosophila* has long been used for genetic research. Originally this was because it bred fast, it was easy to keep, and its chromosomes were relatively big and easily studied under a microscope. Now its genome – the sequence of all the chemical bases along its chromosomes – is also known.

DNA taken from certain people. If a match occurs, it is almost certain that the traces of DNA came from that person.

Since DNA fingerprinting was developed in the 1980s, it has helped to solve thousands of crimes. Similar types of DNA testing can also show how closely people are related.

GENETIC SCREENING
Some people have certain genes which mean they may get a genetic disease as they grow older, or perhaps suffer from a serious illness like cancer. Doctors can now test people's DNA for some of these genes, and warn them in advance. This allows the person to take action, for example, by starting to use certain medicines.

EVIDENCE FOCUS

SPOT THE GUILTY SUSPECT
Try using DNA fingerprinting to spot who carried out this imaginary crime. A house has been burgled but the burglar left behind a few tiny body hairs when squeezing through a part-open window. Police test the DNA in the hair and the DNA of three suspects. The results are shown below. Which suspect is most likely to be the burglar?

	DNA test results
Hair left at crime scene	III IIII I II I I I II
Suspect A	II II II I I III I II
Suspect B	IIII I I II II I III I I
Suspect C	III IIII I II I I I II

ANSWER: Suspect C

37

DNA DEBATES

The science of genetics has brought many amazing discoveries and useful inventions. But does everyone want all this progress? People often argue about how gene science should be used.

◄ Golden rice is a type of GM rice which has been genetically altered to contain extra vitamin A. This could help to prevent blindness in millions of people who have so little food, they do not get enough vitamin A.

SAFE CROPS?

What do people think about GM crops? On one hand, there are possible dangers. Could eating GM plants with different genes, rather than the natural genes for that plant, cause harm to people? Also GM crops designed to kill insect pests or resist weedkillers could damage the environment. These crops might wipe out certain insect species or encourage farmers to use too many chemical weedkillers.

The way that plants breed, by spreading tiny pollen grains and seeds, means that GM crops can spread their new genes to other plants around them. As the new genes 'jump' to other living things they could create new germs, superweeds or superpests. What about the financial cost? Only a few huge companies produce GM crops. As farmers buy the company's GM seeds, they might also have to buy special fertilisers and weedkillers for them – at a higher price than for ordinary versions.

On the other hand, some GM crops could be very beneficial. Those designed to grow in poor or dry soil may one day help people in famine areas. GM food crops altered to contain extra health-giving substances like vitamins could prevent diseases. And pest-resistant GM crops might mean that farmers use fewer pesticides, not more. The arguments about GM crops continue as each side gathers evidence to counteract their opponents.

PLAYING GOD?

Techniques such as genetic engineering, cloning and selecting embryos are sometimes described as 'playing god'. Opponents say that it is not

▶ Protests draw attention to GM crops which might harm the environment. This is partly because gene science is often done by big companies with the main aim of making money. Some people worry that safety could end up less important than the rush for new genetic inventions.

right to create new life in an unnatural way. For some people, it is against their religious or cultural beliefs. Others worry that creating a cloned child would be unfair on the child, who might grow up knowing it had a 'genetic double'. Could 'designer baby' technology give a chance only to genetically perfect people?

SHOULD GENES BE PRIVATE?

If everyone's DNA was tested and the results stored, this might help the police to catch more criminals. But could the information be misused? For example, people with certain unhealthy combinations of genes might find it hard to get life insurance or even a job.

EVIDENCE FOCUS

WHAT DO YOU THINK?

Your class could hold a debate to discuss a genetic issue. Think up a motion – a statement that you will all think about and form views on. For example, a motion might be: 'GM crops are a good thing'.

Split the class into four groups representing four people:

• a poor farmer in a land hit by drought and pests, where GM crops might grow well

• a rich farmer who can afford the best of everything

• the boss of a GM crop company with many employees, who might lose their jobs if the company does badly

• a campaigner for the environment who is concerned about problems GM crops could cause.

Each group researches its topic using books, magazines, the Internet and other resources. The group writes a report of about 200 words putting forward their views on the motion. Then a speaker from each group reads out its report. Finally everyone votes for or against the motion.

WHAT HAPPENS NEXT?

Genetics is one of the most important and fast-moving branches of science. It has the potential to change all our lives. Here are some of the things that gene science could bring in the future.

CLONED CREATIONS

You only need one cell from one living thing to make a clone of that living thing. Some endangered species have already been cloned. If scientists can improve cloning methods, these could provide one last hope for many endangered species such as the tiger, cheetah and giant panda. We might also be able to bring some long-extinct species – perhaps even dinosaurs – back to life using DNA from their preserved remains. Scientists could even create brand new types of creatures and plants by bringing together new combinations of genes from different living things.

▼ In 2005 scientists in Brazil produced two cloned cows, Pora and Potira. They belong to a very rare breed of cow, with less than a hundred individuals left. This is an example of cloning being used to help save endangered breeds and species.

▶ The dodo bird of Mauritius is a worldwide symbol of extinction. The last one died out more than 200 years ago. But by taking DNA from its few actual remains, like bits of skin and bones, could genetic science make it live again? Some people argue that we should try harder to save the threatened wildlife of the present, rather than using money and resources to try to bring back creatures from the past.

DIVIDED SOCIETY?

If genetic alteration for human beings becomes commonplace, it could be used to wipe out many unpleasant diseases and inherited conditions. But if people could select genetic qualities for their children – perhaps choosing a girl or boy – it might lead to a very different society. Children could all end up looking similar, according to the fashions of the time. If people had to pay for the service, wealthy families would have healthier babies than those who could not afford genetic alterations.

DOOM OR A NEW DAWN?

Gene science could lead to a much better life for most people on planet Earth – or it could cause untold disaster. If genetic medicine and GM crops are handled carefully, one day they could banish many diseases and world hunger. But things could go terribly wrong. For example, a genetically engineered virus could escape from a laboratory and kill millions of people. For these reasons and many others, it is important that the science of genetics is carefully regulated.

▶ Genetic engineering might be used to create deadly biological weapons, perhaps for terrorists. Only specially equipped people could survive an attack.

HISTORY FOCUS

PAST PREDICTIONS

A hundred years ago many people said that the newly invented car would never catch on. Then as televisions became common, people warned that no one would listen to the radio again. In the 1990s, as laptop computers spread, some experts said that books would die out. All these predictions about scientific advances were wrong. In the same way, no one can be sure where genetics will lead. Only time will tell.

TIMELINE

Here are some of the main discoveries and milestones in the history of genetics and the progress of gene science.

ABOUT 5000 BC Early farmers realise that some plants and animals pass on diseases to their offspring, and learn to select the strongest individuals for breeding. This is a very early form of genetic modification by allowing only certain animals or plants to have offspring, which is known as selective breeding.

ABOUT 400 BC Ancient Greek doctor Hippocrates (460–377 BC) notices how children receive a mixture of 'qualities' from both their parents.

1630 English doctor William Harvey (1578–1657) guesses that all animals grow from eggs. But he cannot prove this because the reproductive cells cannot be seen – the microscopes of the time are not powerful enough.

1663 English scientist Robert Hooke (1635–1703) uses an improved early microscope to see box-like structures in a cork plant, which he names 'cells'. This is the origin of the biological term 'cell'.

1831–1836 English naturalist Charles Darwin (1809–1882) travels the world. He notices how slight differences – what we now call genetic traits – between animals of the same species give them different chances of survival.

1866 Gregor Mendel (1822–1884), an Austrian monk, publishes his work on how 'hereditary factors' (later called genes) in pea plants are passed on from one generation to the next. His work is ignored for several decades.

1879 German biologist Walther Fleming (1843–1905) uses a new and more powerful type of microscope to observe tiny thread-like shapes (later called chromosomes) inside a cell nucleus. He also sees that these thread-like shapes copy themselves when the cell splits into two cells.

1900 Three different plant experts – Carl Correns (1864–1933) in Germany, Hugo de Vries (1848–1935) in the Netherlands and Erich von Tschermak (1871–1962) in Austria – all repeat Mendel's experiments and prove that he was right.

1902 US cell scientist Walter Sutton (1877–1916) and German cell scientist Theodor Boveri (1862–1915) discover that chromosomes occur in pairs, and that they carry the 'factors' described by Mendel. The 'factors' are renamed genes.

1906 The word 'genetics' is coined for the branch of science dealing with genes.

1910 US biologist Thomas Hunt Morgan (1866–1945) and his team use fruit flies to study how chromosomes and genes are passed on. This work makes fruit flies the main experimental animals for genetics for many years to come.

1944 US scientist Oswald Avery (1877–1955) and his team discover that genes are made of DNA, but they do not know DNA's structure.

1951 English chemist Rosalind Franklin (1920–1958) takes X-ray photographs of DNA. These reveal it has a helical or corkscrew-like shape, but do not show its detailed structure.

1952 US biologists Robert Briggs (1911–1983) and Thomas King (1921–2000) carry out early cloning experiments, successfully creating cloned tadpoles from frog embryos.

1953 US biologist James Watson (born 1928) and English biochemist Francis Crick (1916–2004) discover the detailed double helix structure of DNA and work out how it can copy itself.

1963 Chinese scientist Tong Dizhou creates the first cloned fish, a species of carp.

1966 US biochemist Marshall Nirenberg (born 1927) and Indian-born US biochemist Har Gobind Khorana (born 1922) and their teams crack the genetic code. They work out how the four chemical base units in DNA – A, C, G and T – carry instructions for cells to use. In particular they find how different sequences, each three bases long, are codes for the different chemical ingredients used to build parts of a living thing.

1973 US scientists Stanley Cohen (born 1922) and Herbert Boyer (born 1936) develop a method of taking a section of DNA out of one living thing and inserting it into another. This paves the way for genetic engineering.

1980 US geneticist Martin Cline (born 1934) and his team add genes from other species into mice, to create the first creatures with recombinant DNA – that is, the first genetically engineered animals.

1983 US chemist Kary Mullis (born 1944) invents the polymerase chain reaction (PCR), a method of copying small samples of DNA many times over to give enough DNA for laboratory studies. PCR quickly makes genetics experiments much faster and easier.

1984 English geneticist Alec Jeffreys (born 1950) invents DNA fingerprinting. It is soon used in court as evidence to identify suspects, and becomes an important part of the legal process.

1986 In the USA a type of GM tobacco, one of the first genetically engineered plants, is tested as a crop for the first time.

1990 Scientists in several countries launch the Human Genome Project. It is an international effort to map the order of all the chemical bases along all the strands (chromosomes) of DNA in a human being.

1990 Gene therapy is used for the first time, to treat a four-year-old girl suffering from a disease of the body's self-defence immune system.

1993 GM tomatoes become the first GM food to be widely available to the public, mainly in the USA. However their success is mixed and eventually they are withdrawn.

1996 English geneticist Ian Wilmut (born 1944) and his team create Dolly the sheep, the first mammal to be cloned using a cell taken from another adult mammal.

1997 The complete genome of the *Escherichia coli* bacterium is mapped – the first for any living thing.

1998 Scientists map the complete genome of an animal for the first time – a tiny nematode or roundworm, *Caenorhabditis elegans*.

2000 The first complete genome of a plant is mapped – *Arabidopsis thaliana*, a flowering plant widely studied by geneticists.

2000 Scientists complete the genome map of the fruit fly *Drosophila*.

2000 Early, incomplete versions of the human genome are published.

2001 Geneticists begin to clone endangered species, including a European mouflon (a type of wild sheep) and a gaur (a type of rare cow).

2003 Dolly the cloned sheep dies aged six years, which is half the normal life expectancy for a sheep. She had developed lung disease and joint problems, raising questions about whether cloned animals are healthy.

2003 The complete map of the human genome is published. It consists of 3,200 million chemical bases (As, Cs, Gs and Ts) along all the human chromosomes.

2004 Several countries review their laws about using cloned human embryos in research. Some decide to have fewer regulations. Others make the regulations stricter. Some ban human cloning and similar work completely.

2004 A US company charges $50,000 to clone a pet cat. This is thought to be the first commercial, made-to-order clone.

2005 Scientists find genes linked to increasing numbers of diseases and conditions, including autism, diabetes and several types of cancer, paving the way for new tests and treatments.

GLOSSARY

Alleles Different versions of the same gene.

Atoms The tiny particles making up all objects, substances and materials.

Bacterium A type of tiny living thing, made up of just one cell. It does not have a nucleus (control centre) inside, but still contains genetic material in the form of DNA.

Base A type of chemical unit found in DNA. There are four different bases in DNA.

Budding Growing a branch or bud that breaks off to become a separate living thing, as in some kinds of simple animals.

Carrier Someone who has the gene for an inherited disease in their cells, but who does not suffer from the condition.

Cell membrane The outer 'skin' that surrounds and protects a cell.

Cells Tiny units or 'building blocks' that make up living things, from a single cell in a bacterium to billions of cells in large plants and animals.

Chromosomes Long strands of DNA containing instructions in the form of genes.

Clones Living things that have exactly the same genes as each other, either occurring naturally or produced by scientific methods.

Clotting When blood hardens into a sticky lump, usually when exposed to the air.

Cytoplasm The jelly-like substance that fills most of the inside of a cell.

Designer baby Common but misleading term for a baby which has been chosen for its genes. This happens long before birth, when it is still a tiny embryo. At present this is usually done to avoid a genetic disease.

DNA (deoxyribonucleic acid) A corkscrew-like chemical that forms long strands known as chromosomes, and that carries the information we call genes.

DNA fingerprinting Testing a person's unique DNA patterns. It is often done for similar reasons to taking real fingerprints, such as investigating a crime.

Dominant trait A genetic trait or feature caused by the stronger or more powerful of two alleles (versions of genes).

Double helix The scientific name for DNA's double-stranded, corkscrew-like shape, sometimes misleadingly called a 'spiral'.

Egg cell A female reproductive cell.

Embryo A living thing in the early stages of development. In humans, a baby is called an embryo for the first eight weeks after it begins to develop from a single cell, the fertilised egg.

Endangered species A species of living thing that is in danger of dying out – that is, becoming extinct.

Factors In genetics, an early name for genes, used by the founder of gene science, Gregor Mendel.

Fertilisation When a female egg cell and a male sperm cell join during reproduction, to begin the growth of a new living thing.

Genes Patterns of chemicals inside living things that act as coded instructions, telling the cells how to work and grow, and what to make.

Gene therapy Inserting healthy genes into a living thing to replace missing or faulty genes, in order to cure a genetic condition.

Genetic To do with genes.

Genetic disease A disease that is caused by faulty, missing or extra genes.

Genetic engineering Making changes to the genes of a living thing.

Geneticist A scientist who studies and works with genes and DNA.

Genetics The science of genes.

Genetic trait An inherited feature that is passed on from parents to offspring in their genes.

Genome The complete set of genes for a species of living thing.

GM (Genetically Modified) A description for a living thing, especially a crop or farm animal, that has been genetically altered or engineered.

GM foods GM crops that are used as foods for people or farm animals.

Hormones Natural chemicals in the body that control various processes such as growth.

Junk DNA The DNA in between the genes along a strand of DNA. The name is misleading since recent research shows that some 'junk' DNA is useful.

Meiosis When a cell splits into two, with each resulting cell having only one of each pair of chromosomes.

Mitosis When a cell splits into two, with each resulting cell having both of each pair of chromosomes.

Nucleus The control centre of a cell, containing genes in the form of DNA strands.

Offspring The young or babies of a living thing.

Organelles Tiny parts found inside cells.

Recessive trait A genetic trait or feature caused by the weaker or less powerful of two alleles (versions of genes), when there is no dominant gene to take over.

Reproduce To have offspring, in order to make more living things of the same species.

Reproductive cells Special male and female cells, such as sperm and eggs, which join together to make a fertilised egg cell that grows into a new individual.

Species The scientific name for a kind or type of living thing. All individuals in a species look similar and can breed with each other, but cannot breed with members of other species.

Sperm cell A male reproductive cell.

Virus The tiniest type of germ. It can invade the cells of bigger living things and multiply inside them, causing disease.

FURTHER INFORMATION

Books to read

Genetic Engineering by Sally Morgan (Evans, 2002)

Genetics: The Impact on Our Lives by Paul Dowswell (Hodder Wayland, 2000)

Just the Facts: Genetic Engineering by Steve Parker (Heinemann Library, 2005)

Kingfisher Knowledge: Genes and DNA by Richard Walker (Kingfisher Books, 2003)

Science Essentials: Inheritance and Evolution by Denise Walker (Evans, 2006)

The Usborne Internet-linked Introduction to Genes and DNA by Anna Claybourne (Usborne Publishing, 2003)

What Makes Me Me by Robert Winston (Dorling Kindersley, 2004)

World Issues: Genetic Engineering by Steve Parker (Belitha Press, 2002)

Websites

Science Museum: Who Am I?
www.sciencemuseum.org.uk/exhibitions/genes/index.asp
Interactive online exhibition about genes and how they make you who you are.

The Tech Museum: Understanding Genetics
www.thetech.org/genetics/
The Tech Museum's genetics page, featuring online exhibits such as zooming in on DNA from the starting point of a human hand.

How to Extract DNA from Anything Living
http://gslc.genetics.utah.edu/units/activities/extraction/
Simple instructions for extracting DNA from a cupful of peas and other types of food.

INDEX